2016

are best days

My
BEST
DAY SPORTS I

H-949-645-8109

A Collection of responses from former &
current athletes and coaches

MARK KEYS

Always

Mark Keys

M C C O O L
K E Y S
PRESS

McCool Keys Press
5308 Neptune
Newport Beach, CA 92663
mybestdaybyMarkKeys@yahoo.com

Individual Sales, This book is available through most bookstores or can be ordered directly from McCool Keys Press at the address above.

Quantity Sales. Special discounts are available on quantity purchases by corporations, associations, and others. For details, contact the "Special Sales Department" at the publisher's address above.

Printed in the United States of America.

Library of Congress Cataloging-in-Publication Data is available from the publisher.

ISBN 978-0-9897878-2-6

Cover Design Concept by Mark Keys & Kendall Roderick

Cover design and text design by Kendall Roderick (RMind-Design.com)

The text for this book is set in Century

The author and publisher assume neither liability nor responsibility to any person or entity with respect to any direct or indirect loss or damage caused, or alleged to be caused, by the information contained herein, or for errors, omissions, inaccuracies, or any other inconsistency within these pages, or for unintentionally slights against people or organizations.

Dedication

Sam Dickerson—thanks you for your friendship, kindness
and inspiration; plus the great group of friends you
introduced to me and my family.

In loving memory of David Alan "Bucko" Shaw, the best
friend I could ever have. "He rumbles, he stumbled,
he F·U·M·B·L·E·D."

FORWARD:

While coaching the Los Angeles Lakers' basketball team in the 1970s, I had the honor and privilege of working with the great coach John Wooden while writing a book together regarding basketball techniques and skills. We also conducted several basketball camps together for youngsters and teenagers.

Among his many famous and meaningful quotes, the one that I will always remember most is that "if everyone would magnify their blessings as much as they do their disappointments, they would all be much happier!"

Accordingly, this extremely enjoyable book is a compelling account of how we should live and appreciate our lives every day...and how we can all be much happier for doing so!

— BILL SHARMAN

Hall of Fame NBA Player; Boston Celtics; 4X NBA Champion and former coach, Los Angeles Lakers, Hall of Fame former coach, Los Angeles Lakers

ACKNOWLEDGEMENTS

Thanks go to my wife, Laurie, and wonderful girls, Page and Megan, who always believe in me; my mom and Don Shiel for all their love and support; Frank and Glenell; Thanks to George Yardley, Bill Sharman and John Wooden.

In addition, my appreciation to my supportive friends: Fred Howser & Family, Lt Col. Chuck Bailey, Rick John, the Rogers family, Rev. Jim Birchfield, Vern Fansler, Jon Sweek, Lois & Dick Brockmeyer, Chris and Jane Clark, Ron Lamerton, Blain Skinner, The Helfrich Family, Cass Winstead, Mike Wilsey; Dr. Bellitti, Dr. Rhie, Dr. Stringer, Dr. Carlson, and many more wonderful friends.

INTRODUCTION

In May of 1991, I injured my back while working and was placed on permanent disability. Prior to my first back surgery, I had my picture taken with Magic Johnson of the Los Angeles Lakers. Later, Blain Skinner, a friend of mine who works for the Lakers, was able to get Magic to autograph the snapshot. It made my day.

As a hobby, I began writing other celebrities asking for autographed photos. Their positive result amazed me. During the next several years, while incapacitated with several more back surgeries, knee surgeries, and ankle reconstructions, I collected even more autographs.

One day while walking, I noticed the magnificent beauty of a simple blue sky. Upon returning home, I thought about what a good day it was despite my back problems. I felt great, and it struck me: I wondered what all those people I had been receiving autographs from felt was their "best day"? I began writing letters asking that question. Joey Bishop was the first to reply, and that's how it all began. I received hundreds of responses, and that have evolved into several "My Best Day" books from my collection of inspirational books. I hope you will agree.

—MARK KEYS

Finished reading the letter you had sent and must admit that it has provoked a great deal of thought. Some people would say it was the day the Bears won the Super Bowl in 1985, and still others might argue that it was the day I entered the NFL.

After reflecting upon my career, I feel my best day was the day my son inducted me into the Pro Football Hall of Fame on July 31, 1993, in Canton, Ohio. It meant a great deal to have my son by my side and be a part of that very special occasion.

Thank you for your letter, I wish you both the best.

—WALTER PAYTON
Running Back, Chicago Bears,
NFL Hall of Fame

My Best day was when Coach Frank Leahy offered me a scholarship to play football for Notre Dame. That started a lot of wonderful things for me and I'll always be grateful.

— JOHNNY LUJACK
Football Player, University of Notre Dame, Heisman Trophy Winner

My best day in my athletic career was marching in the opening ceremonies of the 1964 Olympic Games in Tokyo, Japan, as a 20-year old representing the United States of America—my country. I was on the volleyball team, and it was the first time I was ever on foreign soil. It was an experience I will never forget.

—KEITH ERICKSON

San Francisco Warriors, Chicago Bulls, Los Angeles Lakers, NBA Champion 1972

As you can well imagine, leaving UCLA was a very difficult and emotional decision for me after twenty-five years at such a wonderful university. I will never forget all the thoughtfulness expressed by members of the UCLA Bruin family during this time of decision for me. The hardest thing about leaving UCLA was saying goodbye to the great fans, alumni, and supporters that I have come to know and appreciate over the last twenty-five years.

—**TERRY DONAHUE**
Former UCLA Head Football
Coach, General Manager, San
Francisco 49ers

June 19, 1974. Stopping UCLA's 88 game winning streak; Notre Dame 71-UCLA 70, down eleven points with 3:21 left.

—DIGGER PHELPS
Head Basketball Coach, University of Notre Dame, ESPN Commentator

My best day was the first day my cancer started working for me. Being a coach makes me very visible, and so my surgery was well documented in the press.

After surgery, I was recuperating at home and started getting calls from others who were just diagnosed or had family members in the same situation.

I realized on the day of the first call that I could help others through my experience and outlook. I had been empowered to help others regain hope and look positively toward the future. Just my appearance on the sidelines helped others feel they could beat it too.

That was my best day so far...

—DEBBIE RYAN
Basketball Coach, University of Virginia, WNBA Hall of Fame

My best day would have to be the day I was hired at the University of Texas.

—DARRELL ROYAL

Hall of Fame football coach,
University of Texas

My best day was the one when I met my wife. That was 50-years ago and my heart still sings when she walks into the room.

—KEITH JACKSON
NFL/ College Football
Sports Announcer

I have never had a bad day. There is something good in every day. To pick my best day would have to involve looking inward and I don't think like that. My best day would involve making someone else happy, and I try to do that every day; and I think I have done a good job.

— GEORGE YARDLEY
Detroit Pistons, NBA Hall of Fame

I hope it is not too great an assumption to write what someone else might have said was their best day. In this case, it will have to be a best day/worst day...for on May 31st, 1973, in the Indianapolis 500, Lap 33, Swede Savage realized his childhood dream—to lead the Indy 500. However, only moments later his car would crash into the wall coming out of Turn 4 and that crash would eventually lead to his death 33 days later.

—SWEDE SAVAGE
Race car driver, as told by Sheryl Savage Douglas, his widow

One of the best days I ever had was when we played the 49ers in Detroit. I had nearly 500 rushing yards.

—DOAK WALKER

Running Back, Detroit Lions,
5X NFL Pro Bowl, Hall
of Fame

Mr. Williams has had many memorable best days. I guess if you are looking for one of them it would be the day he was inducted into the Hall of Fame. It really meant a lot to Ted to be placed among the best baseball players and some of his dearest friends. Some other (best day) would be related to days spent fishing.

— TED WILLIAMS

MLB Player, Boston Red Sox; 19X All Star, Hall of Fame (Dictated by Ted to Donna Fleischmann, personal assistant)

Probably the best day I had as a Notre Dame Football Player was back in 1953 when we played Southern California (USC) at the Coliseum. Everything went our way after playing a very close-to-the-belt first quarter. During the three quarters, we played extremely well and went on to beat them 48-14. That afternoon, I was a very fortunate halfback because I got to score four touchdowns against the Trojans.

— JOHNNY LATTNER
University of Notre Dame Heisman Trophy Winner, Halfback Pittsburg Steelers, NFL Pro Bowl

Every Sunday!

—GEORGE BLANDA
*Quarterback & Place Kicker,
Chicago Bears, Oakland Raiders, Houston Oilers, NFL
Hall of Fame*

I think my very best day was in 1972 in the play-offs against Pittsburgh. Johnny Bench hit a home run in the 9th inning of the 5th game to tie it. We went on to win in the 9th.

—SPARKY ANDERSON
Hall of Fame MLB Manager;
Cincinnati Reds and
Detroit Tigers

I do believe that my best day must have been the two days each of my sons was born. They are fifteen months apart, and I'll never forget how fantastic each of those two best days were!

—BILL MUSGRAVE
Football Coach, University of Virginia

My too-numerous-to-count best days are when you and others, whether they be family (grandkids, especially now; loved ones; friends; or in my case, football players) realize we are "on the same page," what we are experiencing is special, and that "life has few moments such as this." It happens often if you believe in what you're doing, you believe in the folks you're doing it with, and they believe in you. Then, you will often say: "Life has many moments such as this!"

—**MIKE GIDDINGS**

Former Assistant Coach, USC,
Head Coach University of Utah,
Assistant Coach SF 49ers

Regarding my best day, there are too many to count or think of just one, but if I must, it would be the days my children were born. On July 21, 1996 my daughter was born, and on June 16, 1999, my twin boys were born.

—BOB STOOPS
Head Football Coach, University of Oklahoma

Any day when I am smiling, the sun is out, God is in His Heaven, my children have hope for the brighter tomorrow, and life transcends the mundane, then that is my best day.

—TODD CHRISTIANSEN
Tight End, New York Giants, Oakland Raiders, Announcer, 5X NFL Pro Bowler

Every day that I awaken in good health is my best day. The next day that I wake up with my own health and that of my family will be an even greater day!

—STU LANTZ

NBA Player, San Diego/Houston Rockets, Los Angeles Lakers, New Orleans Jazz, Announcer for the Los Angeles Lakers

My best day was December 30, 1953-the day of my birth. For without existence, nothing else can happen.

Head Football Coach, University of Notre Dame

My best day was when we won our first World Championship in 1966 against the Los Angeles Dodgers.

—BROOKS ROBINSON
Hall of Fame MLB Player;
Baltimore Orioles, 18X All-Star,
2X World Series Champion

Personally, any holiday or wedding when the great majority of our family is together enjoying each other.

Professionally, the day we at USC beat Ohio State in the 1985 Rose Bowl.

—TED TOLLNER
Head Football Coach, USC &
San Diego State University

My best day must have been March 13, 1998. I played at Valparaiso in the NCAA tournament and hit a game winning shot. My dad and brother coached me so it was a great blessing!

—BRYCE DREW
NBA Player, Houston Rockets;
Coach, Valparaiso

As a young aerial gunner on a B-14 Liberator during World War II after coming home from Germany on my thirtieth and final mission. I kissed the ground and it was all over; I survived.

—CHUCK BEDNARIK
Linebacker/Center, Philadelphia Eagles, NFL 8X Pro Bowler, Hall of Fame

Best day(s), partial list: (take your pick)
1. Getting married
2. Two kids
3. TD in Rose Bowl as an 18 year-old freshman
4. Getting out of the Air Force
5. Graduating from USC in 1949
6. Mom at Debutante Ball
7. Making it in the Pro Bowl (SF 49ers)
8. Spending the day with President Ford
9. First Super Bowl

—PAUL SALATA
Receiver, San Francisco 49ers,
"Mr. Irrelevant"

I have had many, many best days: my wedding, the birth of our first child, but probably the best was the day our son came out of a coma after being unconscious for seven days.

—JOE PATERNO
Head Football Coach, Penn State University

My best day was when I got up and played eighteen holes of golf in Vail, Colorado, at the Eagle Springs Golf Course. There was a river on the golf course, so I changed in the parking lot and went fishing for four hours. That was a "perfect day."

—ED MARINARO

Running Back; Minnesota Vikings & New York Jets, Actor "Hill Street Blues"

Best day? Sports: Super Bowl XII January 15, 1978, it was my birthday and I was co-MVP with Harvey Martin. Not a bad day!

—RANDY WHITE
Defensive Tackle, Dallas Cowboys, NFL Hall of Fame

When my daughter was born. Then I realized, and felt, unconditional love. She's given me purpose in life and the desire to be the best I can be in all endeavors.

—MARCELLUS WILEY

Defensive End, Dallas Cowboys, San Diego Chargers, NFL Pro Bowl

Your assignment is a difficult one as we have been blessed with many best days! I think if I have to choose one, it would be the day I married my wife. This December will be thirty-three years of marriage (we married when we were twelve!) Obviously, it has not been easy-we have been through some tough times. However, our relationship has enabled us to work everything out to our satisfaction. We have four wonderful children-all extremely conscientious, hard-working, confident, honest, and bright, Because of them, we feel truly blessed. May the Lord's choicest blessing be with you.

—NORM CHOW
USC & UCLA Assistant Football Coach

Too many days to pick out of best one, but:

Winning the 1938 NFL championship, winning 1956 NFL championship, beating Washington to get to the Super Bowl and winning it, beating San Francisco to get to Super Bowl XXV and upsetting Buffalo in it.

—WELLINGTON MARA
New York Giants, Hall of Fame
President and Owner

Game six of the 1995 World Series.

—GREG MADDUX
MLB Hall of Fame Player;
Chicago Cubs, Atlanta Braves.
LA Dodger, 8X All Star

Here's what I would consider my best day: I was playing Little League in 1967. My dad was sitting in a lawn chair straight-away, center field, behind the fence. I came up to bat, hit my very first ever home run right into my dad's hands. That was my best day ever. I still have that baseball prominently displayed in my home.

—BUCK SHOWALTER

MLB Manager, NY Yankees, Arizona Diamondbacks, Baltimore Orioles, 3X AL Manager of the year

My best day, without a doubt, was the day I married my wife Patti. And that day has turned into forty-nine years of delight. The other best days were when my three children were born. They far outweigh anything to do with football.

—LAVELL EDWARDS
*Head Football Coach, Brigham
Young University*

I am afraid it is impossible to name one best day; I am very fortunate to have many. Winning the British Open in 1969 was certainly one of these, and winning the US. Open in 1970 was also very special. Being captain of the first Ryder Cup Team to win on American soil was another best. Add all that together with being around for the birth of four children; I feel blessed.

—TONY JACKLIN
Professional Golfer

In my business career, my best day was beating the Steelers in Pittsburgh to advance to the Super Bowl.

In my personal life, I would have to say I've had two best days...the days on which my two sons were born.

—DEAN A. SPANOS
President, San Diego Charges

I wish you well in your new endeavor, and I would have to say my best day is every day. Life offers so much, it would be impossible to pinpoint a particular moment; and keeping a positive outlook provides for numerous opportunities. Character and integrity are the goalposts of life. It is difficult to fail when you have those attributes on your team.

—RALPH C. WILSON, JR.
President, Buffalo Bills

I've had so many great days, I would have a hard time picking one. Maybe the Sunday, back in April 1949, when Ann Estock and I decided to run off and get married was the greatest single event to take place in my life. Ann was sixteen yours old, and I was nineteen. We slipped my dad's car away and drove from Birmingham, Alabama, to Risen Falls, Georgia, to be married secretly. We were too young to know better, but we've been married forty-six years. Why did we marry? Because we didn't believe in pre-marital sex (I still don't) and yet we were getting so in love and intimate we had to legalize it. It's probably the best day decision of my life.

—BOBBY BOWDEN
Head Football Coach, Florida State University

Five years ago, February 15, my daughter, Meredith, who had been involved in an automobile accident, was told by her neurosurgeon that she would be paralyzed from the neck down for the rest of her life. That has been the very worst day of my life.

The best days were those leading up to her recovery over the past several years, which leave her now able to walk with the aid of a cane, capable of driving her own car, and leading an independent life.

—BILL SNYDER
*Head Football Coach, Kansas
State University*

The best days of my life are:

When I am relaxing and fishing in the Sierra above Yosemite and can reflect on the good times with my family and friends.

—MIKE WHITE
Oakland Raiders, San Francisco 49ers, KC Chiefs Head Coach

I fondly remember the introductions and game one of the Stanley Cup finals versus the Montreal Canadians at the Forum in 1993. I look forward to experiencing that feeling again soon with the Kings.

—DAVE TAYLOR
Hockey Player,
Los Angeles Kings

I hope my best day is yet to come, and I believe it is. My birth was my best day because without that having happened, nothing else will.

—MIKE DITKA
Chicago Bears, Dallas Cowboys
5X Pro Bowl Tight End; Head
Coach New Orleans
Saints & Chicago Bears

My best day was the Bears versus Redskins game in 1970; I scored the extra point to win the game.

—DICK BUTKUS
Chicago Bears, Linebacker, 8X
NFL Pro Bowl, Hall of Fame

I have been extremely fortunate and blessed during my lifetime that I could give you about 100 best days. But if I could only pick one, I'd say it was January 2, 1997 when the Gators beat FSU 52 to 22; we won the first National Championship in Florida, and my first time as a head coach in what makes a championship so special is that you have so many people to share with: your family, your coaches, players, and everyone I call a friend.

—STEVE SPURRIER
*Head Coach, Washington
Redskins, South Carolina &
University of Florida*

In my "real" life: The day I married my wife. Every day thereafter has been filled with a meaning and joy that only mutual love can bring into the world...which lead to the birth of our daughter.

In my "sports" life: Every day my dad's car turned the corner home after work. It meant we were going to shoot baskets together until it was time to come in for dinner.

I remember the day...

I had to jump on his back to guard him, but it had no impact whatsoever...

I finally beat him one-on-one...

Playing with so many friends over so many years when he finally "hung 'em up" on his 70th birthday and he still had a pretty good hook.

—CASEY JONES
European Professional Basketball Player

You ask me what my best day was and I think I would have to choose a day in 1983. I was attending North Carolina State when we advanced to the national championships in Albuquerque. I have always had a close relationship with my mom and although her fear of flying would prevent her from attending the game I knew she would be there in spirit.

When our team fought hard through a tough game and was regarded with the victory it was even more special when I looked up into the stands and saw my mom's face. She looked so happy and proud of me that in the midst of the team's celebration, I ran directly into the stands and gave her a big hug.

My mom has always been a wonderful teacher and source of inspiration. In attending the game that day, as in so many other days, she inspired me to always face my fears and challenges head on.

—SIDNEY LOWE

Head Basketball Coach, Vancouver Grizzlies, Assistant Minnesota Timberwolves, NBA Player Detroit Pistons, Charlotte Hornets

My best day in recent years was December 6, 1997, when Tennessee won the Southeastern conference championship.

—PEYTON MANNING
Quarterback, Indianapolis Colts and Denver Broncos, 14X NFL Pro Bowl

I have been very fortunate during my lifetime. I have a wonderful family, a wife for fifty-three years, and all blessed with good health, this has been possible due to many "best days".

The same holds true in my life in the NFL. A lot of people have been responsible for those best days.

Just for me personally, I would probably have to say that all my best days were capsulated in the day I was inducted into the Professional Football Hall of Fame. I thank all those who made that best day possible.

—TEXAS SCHRAM
Hall of Fame, NFL Executive
Dallas Cowboys

My best day was the day Nellie said, "yes" and later, "I do"

—JOHN WOODEN
*Hall of Fame Head Basketball
Coach UCLA*

My retirement at the Boston Garden was "personally" my most significant moment; winning our first Championship in April 1957 (1956/57 season) was the most important team moment.

—**BOB COUSY**

Coach, Boston Celtics, 6X NBA Champion, Hall of Fame

My best day was probably in 1980 when we beat UCLA for the National Championship in Indianapolis. We had been to the Final Four twice and had not won. Everyone was saying, "Crum can't win the big one." That really got the monkey off my back.

—DENNY CRUM
Head Basketball Coach, University of Louisville

My best day is a simple one. November of my junior year of high school, I accepted Christ into my life. This decision has made each day forward very meaningful and special.

—STEVE ALFORD
Head Basketball Coach, University of Iowa, UCLA

My best days were the seventh game of the World Championship Series with the Washington Bullets in 1978, and game six with the Lakers in 1985. We beat the Celtics. Other than that, the Olympic Gold Medal in 1976 stands alone by itself.

—MITCH KUPCHAK

NBA Player, Washington Bullets, L.A. Lakers; General Manager Los Angeles Lakers, 3X NBA Champion

I have been blessed to have so many best days, so I'll give you a few. When I first met my late husband, Don Drysdale, at the Superstars. When we got engaged and he gave me a ring. When we got married. And the three times we brought a new life into this world! A part of both of us. Those were my best days.

Sports? Competing in the 1976 Olympics, and winning a silver medal for our country. And every competition representing our country and winning medals. UCLA! Watching my brother David play all four years for Coach Wooden. And winning the National Title his senior year. (Also, in high school when his team won CIF.)

When our 1978 team won the Women's National Title, and being named player-of-the-year. After having been named a four-time All-American. Graduating from UCLA! Watching Don in 1984 get elected into the Baseball Hall of Fame. Nine years later, I received the same honor for Basketball Hall of Fame (and having all my family in Springfield to share in such a special time). Signing with the Indiana Pacers back in 1979 and having a tryout. I also have a lot of good days ahead of me!

— **ANN MEYERS-DRYSDALE**
Guard, US Olympic Team, New Jersey Gems, Hall of Fame basketball player and announcer

During my 39 years of teaching and coaching, I woke up each morning, prepared for my day, and wondered what challenge that day would hold. Fridays were never considered with the thought "TGIF" and Mondays never came fast enough. I loved the classroom, I loved the gym, and my office was my second home. I had a varied schedule: Freshman comp, advanced comp, sociology of sports and psychology of sport. My students came from every walk of life, with varying interests. How could a day not be a challenge?

Every day of teaching was a best day. Certainly I had particular best days; graduation days, my marriage day, the days our children were born. These are all best days. More specifically, the day I was contacted to be director of player development in the CBA, the Continental Basketball Association, was a best day. This offer enabled me to work full time in basketball, so I retired from teaching at Orange Coast College.

When I was a child growing up in New York, living near Madison Square Garden, I had a dream of being in the NBA (The BAA when I was just a kid). I realized as a teenager I wouldn't "play" in the NBA, but maybe I could get there as a coach, or as a scout. (Yes, this thought crossed my mind as a teenager.) Can you imagine the reaction on

my heart the day the Portland Trailblazers offered me a full-time position in their organization
as a player scout? In some ways, maybe that was
my best day.

—HERB LIVSEY

*Teacher and Professional
Scout, Portland Trailblazers,
Denver Nuggets*

In remembering all my years in racing, I would find it very difficult to pick one day as my best day. I have been very fortunate to have many a best day in my career.

If I had to pick one day though it would be the Saturday that Sunday Silence won the Breeder's Cup Classic, after winning the Derby and the Preakness. A close second would be when Ferdinand slipped through to the rail and won the Kentucky Derby.

—CHARLES WHITTINGHAM
Hall of Fame Horse Trainer

It was been difficult to write about a best day, as I have been very fortunate to have many best days.

The day I was married; the day my first son was born; the first Steeler Super Bowl victory and all the Steeler Super Bowls; my first game at North Catholic when I scored six touchdowns.

But, I would have to say my very best day was in 1989 when the Steelers beat Denver to put us in the AFC Championship and several hours later my first grandson was born on Christmas day— that was the best day.

I hope you all will have many best days.

—DAN ROONEY
*President, Pittsburg Steelers,
NFL Hall of Fame*

One of my best days, I recall, was against the Baltimore Colts in November, 1960, when I was playing for Detroit Lions. I didn't start but entered the game in the fourth quarter with the score 8-3 in favor of the Colts. I threw a forty-yard touchdown pass to Hop Cassidy who caught the pass and ran into the goal post for the six points.

Next series, we kicked a field goal to make the score Detroit 13-Colts 8 with two minutes fifty-three seconds on the clock. Johnny Unitas took Baltimore down the field and threw a thirty-four yard touchdown pass to Lenny Moore to take the lead 15-13. Colts kicked off to the Lions with fourteen second on the clock, and we returned to our own thirty-five yard line. I then threw a pass to our tight end, Jim Gibbons, with ten seconds remaining, and he went sixty-five yards, scoring the winning touchdown, Detroit Lions 20-Baltimore Colts 15. It was the last play of the game.

—EARL MORRALL
Quarterback, Detroit Lions, 2X
Pro Bowler

The date was august 17, 1968. I was suspended in a parachute, slowly drifting down onto the Gulf of Tokin, just off the coast of North Vietnam, having been ejected from a burning fighter jet. I realized that this was my last combat mission. I had survived Vietnam. I was going home.

As I felt the fragile Voyager finally come to a stop in the middle of Muroc Dry Lake with tens of thousands of supporters and friends cheering and congratulating us, the realization began to penetrate my fatigued conscience that we had done it- -we had flown around the earth without stopping and without refueling. we had just conquered aviation's last milestone.

December 14-23, 1986

26,366 miles9 days, 3 minutes, 44 seconds

Edwards Air Force Base to Edwards Air Force Base

—DICK RUTAN
Voyager Pilot

I have been richly blessed throughout my life to have a loving and supportive family and good friends who have always been there for me during the good and difficult times. I've had the opportunity to coach some outstanding teams that have won championships. The most memorable may have been one of my least talented teams during my first year at BYU. We were on the road at New Mexico, and they had won four straight at home. We played an almost perfect game and won going away. The next morning at 8:00 A.M., the "sports babe" had me on the phone and wanted to hear about the miracle game. Twelve-months earlier I was driving the team van and sweeping the floors at the junior college. That day, we made the lead article in USA Today, and I was talking on national radio. One day later we defeated UTEP in triple overtime to qualify for the WAC tournament.

That was a special group of young men who never quit and stayed positive to the end.

—**STEVE CLEVELAND**
Head Basketball Coach,
Brigham Young University

I can tell you that my best day has not yet arrived (written March 14, 1996). It will come this June 7th when my wife, Barbara, who has worked for many years, will graduate from the University of Utah. It will be very pleasing to me because I enjoy myself most when I see people who have worked very hard get their just rewards.

—FRANK LAYDEN
President, Utah Jazz

I had a brother that was blind, and he used to say every day was a good day! My best day is: yesterday, today, tomorrow.

—DAVE WILCOX
Linebacker, San Francisco 49ers, 7X NFL Pro Bowl, Hall of Fame

My best day was the day I married my wife, Karen.

—BOB KNIGHT

Head Basketball Coach, Army,
Indiana, Texas Tech University

I was going to Lebanon High School in 1966; Semi-State afternoon game against Logansport. I scored 20 points in the last quarter, 9 for 10 from the field in that period. We won the game, and I had 47 points with 15 rebounds.

—RICK MOUNT
Indiana Pacers, ABA Championship 1972

Big upset in 1988, Georgia Tech vs. Oklahoma; being in the stands when (my son) Scooter made the winning free throws; NBA Championship in 1975.

—RICK BARRY

Golden State Warriors, Houston Rockets NBA Hall of Fame

It is impossible to pick one best day in a lifetime when you consider your family, career, and various interests. each stage of my life has brought me both great joy and, to some degree, sorrow. How could I compare or equate the joy of the birth of any one of my children against the close game where a win was seemingly unattainable, but happens? How can you balance the thrill of accepting an Olympic Gold Medal with the joy of a long, happy marriage or fulfilling relationship with family members and friends?

It can't be done.

Today is my best day. May your today be your best day too.

—OSCAR ROBERTSON
Milwaukee Bucks, Cincinnati
Bucks, NBA Hall of Fame

My best day was my college graduation. The joy of accomplishment after working so hard was overwhelming. I realized I could accomplish anything in life, but it started with me!

—WENDY PALMER

Orlando Miracle, San Antonio Stars, WNBA

By far my best day was actually two days—both days being the births of my two sons. The two days were different however. My first son's birth day was hectic. My wife didn't know she was in labor. I had just gotten out of a leg cast, which I had been in for three months, and was on crutches. It was in the afternoon; traffic getting to the hospital was heavy; labor at the hospital was very quick (less than two hours). Not an easy delivery, but what a great feeling when he did emerge. Instant love and joy.

Number two son's birth day was much different. We drove to the hospital at 4:00 A.M., no traffic, a light snow falling. It was so peaceful and serene; the delivery was much smoother; the labor had not been long, and we knew what to expect. A natural delivery; the same love and joy instantly. Without a doubt, those were my two best days.

—GEORGE IRVINE
ABA Player, Denver Nuggets,
Detroit Pistons; Indiana Pacers
Head Coach

I've had so many good days that it's almost impossible to choose one. I feel I've been very fortunate my entire life and extremely so now, to be doing exactly what I am.

I guess my best day was in March of 1991, when we beat Arkansas and were assured of going to the 1991 Final Four. We were down 12 at halftime and outscored Arkansas by 24 points in the second half to win by 12. It was really the establishment of our program, and I hope we can continue to keep it at this level. What made the day even more appealing, though, was that my entire family was in Charlotte with me, which included my mother, wife, 19-year-old son, and 11-year-old daughter. They were so excited after the game and wanted to make sure they would get to go. That's about as good as it can get.

—ROY WILLIAMS
Head Basketball Coach,
University of North Carolina

A best day really is any day that I get to go to practice to teach and coach bright, motivated, talented young women who are following their athletic and academic dreams.

I really do believe I have one of the best jobs in the world!

— **JODY CONRADT**
Player, Baylor, Women's Basketball Coach, University of Texas NCAA Champions 1986

It was a thrill and a great honor to be doing the Laker broadcasts while filling in for Chick.

As for my best day, like many people I have had several. But my most recent best day happened just two weeks ago when my mother was given a clean bill of health after undergoing an arduous course of chemotherapy. That was a best day for sure.

—PAUL SUNDERLAND
US Olympic Gold Medal Volleyball Team 1974, Announcer, Los Angeles Lakers

Every day our oldest daughter greets me with her head of tossled hair and gentle, dimple-laden smile...

Every day our middle son sees something I assume he cannot, for he is visually impaired...

Every day our youngest daughter needs me to hold her...

Every day, all day, of this blessed life.

—TRACY LONGO RATH
Player, USC Women's Basketball
Champions, 1982 - 1984

I was lucky enough to marry an astonishingly level-headed woman at a time when I knew very little about life and the value of good relationships. She had no pretensions and a multitude of great friends. During our first five years of marriage we had three little boys; John, Joe and Pete, who were the joy of our lives. Sheila, my wife, was a great mom, always knowing just how to handle the little munchkins. They began to grow up sound of mind and straight of limb, and I marveled at how she handled their growth and attitudes.

I thought to myself, wouldn't it be great for a little girl to have Sheila as a mom? Soon she was pregnant again and I somehow sensed that this one would be a little girl, but I was afraid to say anything to anyone about it for fear of jinxing the deal.

In those days the dads were not allowed in the delivery room so I waited outside for the news of the birth. Sure enough, on May 31, 1968, the doctor came out and told me that we had a little girl. My dream came true and a wonderful little girl would have Sheila for a mom. I was overjoyed—in fact, I cried because I knew the relationship that would surely happen.

That was more than 30-years ago and every hope I had has happened. They are so close. Not to the point of something maudlin, but in the most beautiful way. Our daughter, Tracy, is happily married, living in Montana, far from us, with a little girl Josie, nearly two and another little girl on the way.

Sheila is her best friend and, in fact, was Tracy's matron of honor at her wedding, a dream come true.

Tracy's birth was my happiest moment and it happened on my best day.

—DANNY ROGERS
President/CEO, Goodwill Industries of Orange County, USC Basketball 1957; Men's Basketball Coach, UCI

I. I believe winning our first NBA World Championship with the "Boston Celtics" in the 1956-1957 season was probably the most happy and meaningful day of my career, as it was the first championship of the great Celtic dynasty that has never been matched by any other team in any other professional sport.

II. I guess being inducted into the Basketball Hall of Fame in May, 1975 was probably the most individual honor I have received.

—BILL SHARMAN

Hall of Fame Player, NBA, 4X National Champion Boston Celtics; Hall of Fame Coach, 1972 NBA Champions Lakers, and 5X NBA Champion as Laker Administrator

My best day golf-wise was the 4th round of the 1959 Masters.

That day I birdied five of the last holes for a score of 66 and I won the 1959 Masters!

—ART WALL
Professional Golfer

Many thanks for your inspiring letter asking for the best day of my life so far.

I truly have to say that between my family life and my basketball life, there have been too many to name. I am a fortunate man and I am thankful for that.

I will leave you with an old Irish toast to the New Year..."May your right hand always be reaching out for friendship and not in want."

—JIM CALHOUN
Hall of Fame Head Basketball Coach, University of Connecticut

I must admit, it is difficult to select only one memory, since I have been blessed with many wonderful experiences so far during this lifetime.

One that ranks highly is the day I met my wife, Cindy. Our meeting profoundly influenced the course of my life, and I believe that I have been able to draw strength from the stability of our marriage during all of the challenges that I have encountered throughout my career in professional basketball.

I also feel that the days my children were born are among my best-day memories. Nothing can compare to the long-awaited appearance of an infant: They enter the world as such beautiful little people and before you know it, they grow into wonderful, bright, enchanting individuals. It is truly an amazing transformation to watch.

—PAUL WESTPHAL
NBA Player, 1974 Champion
Boston Celtics, Head
Coach Phoenix Suns,
Pepperdine University

My best day—it had to be a year and almost three months ago when doctors saved my life at a basketball game. It's great to get a second chance.

—CHARLIE COLES
Basketball Coach, University of Miami, Central Michigan

My Best Day was and is every day I get to spend with my family and friends doing the things I love most.

—LARRY ROBINSON
Hall of Fame Hockey Player,
Montreal Canadians, LA Kings

My best days—the day I married my wife, Leslie, and the births of our three children, Dristin, Lisa and Kyle.

But let me pass along another thought; it came from my mentor, Coach John Wooden. He said, "You haven't had a perfect day until you've done something for someone else for which they could never repay you."

So, when I've done something for someone else for which they could never repay me—then I've had a perfect day and perhaps my best day.

—BRAD HOLLAND
Player, 1980 NBA Championship Lakers, Head Coach, University of San Diego Basketball

My best day was Easter 1961 when at a Billy Graham service in Barton, Florida I surrendered my life to Jesus. My best baseball day was when I was inducted into the Baseball Hall of Fame in Cooperstown.

—ERNIE HARWELL
Baseball Hall of Fame Announcer, Baltimore Orioles, Detroit Tiger

My best day was when I was fifteen years old and I got my first announcing job at a 250-watt radio station. I used this story as a prologue to my book, What Makes Winners Win.

—CHARLIE JONES
NFL Hall of Fame Announcer

It's impossible to list ONE best day! Nearly all of them have been good..."I took an hour to look at a flower and a day to examine a shell. A week went by while I watched the sky. O' God has treated me well."

—BOB SHEPPARD
New York Yankees Announcer

I wasn't there for my best day. It was my son's best day and therefore mine. Conner was born on May 19, 1996 about two hours after his twin brother, Creighton, died at birth. They each weighed about a point and a half. Conner fought hard. He got big—nine pounds. And one day during his six months inside Maine Medical Center he got to take a stroller ride with his mom, my wife, Laura. His joy that day, not his death another day, is how I remember him.

—KENNY MAYNE
ESPN sportscaster

Wow...my best day; that's a tough one. After calling races for 28 years I honestly cannot recall a best day.

My imaginary best day would be one in which all the horses came back safe and sound; a crowd of 60,000 saw a grade one race that ended in a three-way photo finish; and an up-and-coming three-year old won a race so sensationally that I thought I had just seen the next Kentucky Derby winner.

—TREVOR DENMAN
Horse Racing Announcer

Two days that were my best without question were the day I was married and the day my daughter was born. I do have to mention two other days that I will always remember. The day the hostages walked off of the plane on American soil, which I covered for ABC News, and the first shuttle launch, which I also covered for ABC news. I'll never forget the emotions evident that day in Washington or the feel of the TV trailer vibrating because of the propulsion launch.

—CHET FORTE
*Eleven-time Emmy winner and
former director, ABC Monday
Night Football*

Every day I do a game—it's the best!
Awesome baby!

—DICK VITALE
Coach, Detroit Pistons, Sports
Announcer; NBA Hall of Fame

My best day would have to be the day I left the Indian River Hospital in Vero Beach, Florida after a stay of four months, including six weeks in critical condition in intensive care due to a traffic accident.

That day, July 24, 1990 is my best day because my doctors told my wife that I had only an eight percent chance of surviving the second surgery.

—JAMIE JARRIN
*Spanish Broadcaster; Los
Angeles Dodgers*

The best day of my life would be October 22, 1980 the date of the parade down Broad Street to old JFK Stadium to celebrate the 1980 Championship Philadelphia Phillies.

To witness the hundreds and thousands of fans lined up the length of Broad Street to the overflowing 100,000-seat JFK Stadium was breathtaking. It was a true love-in of Philadelphia fans and their championship team. I was honored to emcee the ceremonies at JFK Stadium. Philadelphia fans are known to be tough, but on this day it was truly a love affair of a city's only World Championship baseball team and an entire city's wonderful baseball fans.

—HARRY KALAS
Baseball Announcer,
Philadelphia Phillies

My best day was when my roller hockey team, the Los Angeles Blades of Roller Hockey International (RHI), defeated our archrivals, the Anaheim Bullfrogs for the first time. It took a few years for us to defeat them on their home territory so the victory was much sweeter. I actually believe the sky was bluer the next day.

Because I belong to a family where sports are our religion I had several best days in mind, and they all included victories in sports. The "Miracle on Manchester" Kings hockey game, on April 10, 1982, where the Kings came back from being down 5-1, before defeating Edmonton in OT 6-5. The 1985 NBA Championship game where the Lakers defeated the Boston Celtics on the parquet floor in Boston Garden! Finally, winning my first championship in 1990 as a general manager of the Los Angeles Strings of World Team Tennis. All of these thoughts came into my head (as a matter of fact, I have enjoyed reliving each moment writing this letter to you!) after reading your request. That is what happens when sports and your life are one.

—JEANIE BUSS
President, Los Angeles Lakers

What was my best day? Now let me think—I'd have to say it was the night I fought my last fight. After having guys take whacks at you for 18 years, (that's how long I was a fighter), to say to the world, "goodbye, that's enough" what a great thrill.

—ART ARAGON
Boxer, "Golden Boy"

The final round in the Masters 1937 when I shot 32 on the last nine, to win by two. Also, the 1945 PGA Championship at Moraine Country Club in Dayton. It was my 9th tournament win in a row.

—BYRON NELSON

Hall of Fame
Professional Golfer

Final round, "63" at Oakhurst!"

— JOHNNY MILLER
Hall of Fame Professional
Golfer and Analyst

It would be very difficult for me to say what was the best day I've ever experienced. There are so many outstanding days in my life that I cannot possibly pick one out.

I have to think of the time our children were born or when they were married or when we found out my wife did not have cancer; but probably the greatest day of my life would be when I decided to turn it over to Jesus Christ.

—LOU HOLTZ
Head Football Coach, Notre Dame, University of South Carolina, ESPN Announcer

Every day is opening day with me.

—JACK BURKE
Professional Golfer

My best day has been hearing from you [Mark Keys].

— DON JANUARY
Professional Golfer

My best day was the day I married my wife, 66-years ago in Los Angeles. My second best day was when I won the Los Angeles Open, my first of 30 wins on tour. My third best day was when I got the ring for my induction into the PGA World Hall of Fame in 1992, to go along with my other six Hall of Fames.

—HARRY "LIGHTHOUSE" COOPER
Hall of Fame Professional Golfer

First of all every day I wake up is a best day.

I played the Asian tour for eight years on and off. I was so lucky to have great Pro-Am partners, but one in particular let me into their world for one day. I was paired with the King of Malaysia from the region of Perak. He was the kindest man and very open with me. He made me feel at home, well sort-of, except for the machine-gun carrying secret service/bodyguards everywhere. That experience was the start of a "best week" for me.

My sister Cathy qualified for the U.S. Women's Open two-years ago. It was held in Chicago, Illinois. I decided to go back and give her my support. The day of her first round on the first tee, with the announcer introducing her - that was a best day.

—NANCY MOCKETT
Professional Golfer

Every day I put on a baseball uniform was my best day.

—GENE MAUCH
*MLB Player, Brooklyn Dodgers,
Boston Red Sox, Manager Min-
nesota Twins, California Angeles*

October 3, 1951: Giants-Dodgers playing for the pennant. Last of the 9th inning, Dodgers are winning 4-2. One out, 2 men on. I got up and hit "the shot heard 'round the world" to win the pennant 5-4.

—BOBBY THOMSON
MLB Player, New York Giants,
Milwaukee Braves, 3X All Stars

I have had a blessed life and feel like every day is my best day. Giving my life to Jesus Christ when I was 9-years old was my best day! Getting married to my wife was next, then the birth of my children were wonderful days! Signing with the New York Yankees at 17-years old wasn't that bad either!

—REX HUDLER
MLB Player, New York Yankees,
California Angels and Announcer

The day I got my own locker and Major League uniform with my name on it; it was a day my prayers, as a kid, were answered.

—JOHNNY VANDERMEER
MLB Player Cincinnati Reds, Chicago Cubs, 4X All Star

Every day is my best day. Every day presents a new challenge and another opportunity to grow and to make a difference and to enjoy the blessing of life.

—**LLOYD CARR**
Football Coach, University of Michigan

I think the best day for me this past season was meeting with the senior players at the Fiesta Bowl and having a true sense of concern and caring among that group of players, as well as preparing to play the game. It illustrated to me that the past four years had been meaningful in their lives and that they care very much about each other and this football program.

—TOM OSBORNE

U.S. Congressman; former head football coach, University of Nebraska

In 12 seasons with the Dodgers our team played in 6 World Series so there were many great days. My very best was in 1953, October 2nd against the Yankees—winning 3-2 on a homerun by Campanella in the 8th. I had 14 strikeouts—a World Series record. Among them was Mantle 4 times, and the final, Johnny Mize, a great hitter.

—CARL ERSKINE

MLB Player, Brooklyn/ Los Angeles Dodgers, 1954 All Stars, 1955 World Series

The 1972 playoffs against the Pittsburgh Pirates. I hit a home run in the 9th inning of the 5th game to tie it, and went on to win the game in the 9th. Also, my retirement game, I hit a home run.

—JOHNNY BENCH
MLB Player, Cincinnati Reds,
14X All Star, Hall of Fame

My best day was being on the mound October 1, 1967 when the Boston Red Sox won the American League Pennant at Fenway Park. We beat the Twins 5-3 and 30,000 people came on the field to celebrate the victory.

—JAMES LONBORG
MLB Player, Boston Red Sox,
1967 All Star

My best day—Saturday, June 14, 1962 versus the New York Yankees in Cleveland Stadium. My fourth hit that day was a two-run homerun in the last of the 9th that won the game 9-8. That victory in front of 65,000 fans tied the Indians for the American League lead with the Yankees.

—JERRY KINDALL
MLB player, Cleveland Indians,
Chicago Cubs, Minnesota Twins

Really a tough question to ask; I always thought my days were good. Just putting on the Major League uniform every day of the season were the best days. One series in Boston over a weekend I drove in 14 runs, hit some homers, and had a good weekend. One day in Washington I hit my 6th straight home run in 6 straight games to tie the American League record. It took 17 innings but I did it off Al Aber of Detroit. Had a wonderful career; wouldn't change anything.

—ROY SIEVERS
MLB player; Washington Senators, Chicago White Sox, 5X All-Star

Driving in the winning run 1975 World Series in the 9th inning.

—JOE MORGAN

MLB Hall of Fame Player; Cincinnati Reds, SF Giants, Philadelphia Phillies; 10X All-Star, & MLB Announcer

My best day was in June of 1975, I went 5-6 with three home runs, one triple, one single and ten RBI's. The only out I made was a line out to second. We won 15-1.

—FRED LYNN

MLB Player; Anaheim Angels,
Boston Red Sox, Detroit Tigers,
9X All-Star

Max tells me his best day was when he joined the Cleveland Indians in 1946. Lou Boudreau signed him from an exhibition game against the Indians. When he joined in '46 as first base coach, it was great. In Cleveland Stadium where 80,000 people honored Babe Ruth, Ty Cobb and Tris Speaker, he had the honor of shaking hands with these immortals.

He performed for two innings of every baseball game to standing ovations and stayed on for 1946 and 1947.

Max has had to retire this year, (1995) much to his dismay; for baseball has been his life. After 50 years it isn't easy to say goodbye.

—MAX PATKIN
Baseball entertainer (as told by his sister, Ruth Cohen)

My best day on the baseball field would be difficult to categorize. One that stands out in my memory is the first time I hit my 50th home run in 1947. It was a goal I never dreamed possible in only my second year in the Major Leagues, especially since I had just three home runs at the end of May that year.

—RALPH KINER
Hall of Fame MLB Player;
Pittsburg Pirates, Chicago
Cubs, 6X All-Star

My best day was game five of the 1964 World Series. In the 10th inning I hit a three-run home run to win the game.

—TIM McCARVER
MLB Player, St. Louis Cardinals, Boston Red Sox, 2X All-Star, World Series Champion; MLB Announcer

Every day when I wake up I cherish every moment.

—VIDA BLUE

Hall of Fame MLB Player; Oakland A's, SF Giants, Kansas City Royals, 6X All-Star, 3X World Series Champion

My best day—I would probably have to say it would be getting the last out in the 7th game of the 1972 World Series.

—ROLLIE FINGERS

Hall of Fame MLB Player;
Oakland A's, San Diego Padres,
7X All-Star, 3X World
Series Champion

The 1951 World Series--Giants versus Yankees. I got four straight hits and stole home for the first time in 30 years. When I came up for the fifth time, I lined out to Joe Collins, the Yankees' first baseman; the ball was hit real hard and Joe was lucky to catch it.

—MONTE IRVIN

Hall of Fame MLB Player; New York Giants, Chicago Cubs, World Series Champion

My best day: paying back my parents for college tuition.

—MARK PRIOR
*MLB Player; Chicago Cubs,
All-Star*

I have always believed in this statement: yesterday is history, tomorrow is a mystery, today is a gift from God.

That's why my best day is today (always).

—**MORGAN WOOTEN**
Legendary High School Basketball Coach, Dematha Catholic High School

Nothing can compare to the day of my wedding, 68-years ago and still going.

—BRUCE BENNETT
Olympic shot-putter and Actor;
Mildred Pierce, Dark Passage

I really have two best days and it is hard to distinguish between the better one. The first best day is the day I gave birth to my eight-year old son, and he was healthy. The second best day is every day I wake up. (God could have called me home in the middle of the night.) I don't think people realize how blessed they are to be able to wake up alive. These are the best days for Gwen.

—GWEN TORRENCE
Olympic Track Star

I guess any day I wake up has to be a best day so there have been many of them. To pick one is difficult, but after two good marriages, two terrific daughters and three healthy eyes-up grandkids— plus four Olympic gold medals, four world records and six national championships, my best day perhaps is as follows:

I was driving to Vermont, New Hampshire and the Berkshires during the autumn leaf change when I read that the city of Braintree, Massachusetts was having an all-comers track meet. This was 1976 and at that time I had been retired for eight years from competition.

I decided to drive on over and once there to throw with the collection of old and young athletes. I had to borrow a pair of throwing shoes and a discus, pay my 50 cents to compete; but once I entered the ring for my first throw it was as if I had come home. Distance didn't matter, nor did placing well, but the feeling of this is where I wanted to be dug in deeply--the quest for the next games. I stayed in competition 12 more years after that day, and while I never won another gold medal, I pushed the boundaries of age and capability as far as anyone has. To say the least—a best day.

—AL OERTER
4X Olympic gold medalist;
Track and Field

131

To answer your question, aside from the three days that each of my daughters were born, I'd have to say my best day was when Alysheba won the Derby in 1987. There is nothing like the first one.

—CHRIS McCARRON
Hall of Fame Professional
Horse Jockey

My best day in racing was the Kentucky Derby in 1974; Cannonade and the 100th Kentucky Derby were something special.

—WOODY STEPHENS
Hall of Fame Horse Trainer

The biggest thrill was my first Derby, Lauren in 1938; I never thought I would win one, let alone five.

—EDDIE ARCARO
Hall of Fame Horse Jockey

The last race I rode.

—JOHNNY LONGDEN
*Hall of Fame Horse Jockey and
Triple Crown winner*

My best days in racing were:
1. Winning the Kentucky Derby with Pleasant Colony.
2. The Preakness with the same horse.
3. Winning the Breeders Cup Classic and the Juvenile for fillies the same day.
4. Winning with my first mount here in the USA.

—JORGE VELASQUEZ
Hall of Fame Horse Jockey

My best day was in October 1988: I was riding a horse here at Santa Anita who had been racing primarily in Seattle prior. The trainer was a man named Robert Leonard, he trained as a hobby, he was a full-time Pilot for Northwest Orient; usually he would call me before his races from another country with riding instructions. Back to the day, the race was the Norfolk Stakes, a Grade I for two-year olds. It rained hard all day and the track came up sloppy. We were going to scratch if I felt he didn't like the going during the parade to post. Well, as you can guess, he came from far back to win going away and won, it was exciting! As you know every day is your and my best day. This is just one of many best days but it really stands out to me!

—**JOE STEINER**
Professional Horse Jockey

My best day would be the first training session back with the national team after being cut. Knowing that every minute, sweating, in pain, meant something. It reinforced to me that I still had more to give, even when I was struggling with the idea of never playing for the national team again.

I am constantly grateful for the support of my family, friends and coaches for never giving up on me either. My best day was one sunny afternoon spent on the soccer field wearing proudly the colors of the bravest nation in the world.

—BRANDY CHASTAIN
Soccer Player; Unites States
World Cup winning team

My best day was July 4, 1997 when I married the greatest person I have ever met, Mark Henderson. We had 270 people from all over the world celebrating with us in Squaw Valley. My best friend's dad and sister sang "You've got a Friend," and our two club swim coaches read poems. It was outside on a beautiful, perfect 80-degree day. We danced and sang some more, into the wee hours. I couldn't believe that we got that many of our friends together for one day when it is so hard to get together with one just for dinner. It was the best day and will be (maybe) until we have kids!

—SUMMER SANDERS
1992 Olympic 2X Gold
Medalist Swimmer

Without question my best day was the day after a successful delivery of my prematurely-born daughter. The doctor said she'd be fine, and now 13-years later, she is.

Athletically my best day was the final day of the 1974 NCAA Swimming Championships. My school, USC, defeated the University of Indiana with a final score of 339-338, thanks in part to my three individual titles and three American records (in three swims).

—**JOHN NABER**
Olympic 5X Gold Medal Swimmer and Announcer

My best day was winning the Olympic gold medal in platform diving at the 1948 London Olympics. The 16 years of dreaming to be an Olympic diving champion seemed like 16 seconds. I wanted to show the world that freedom to pursue one's dream as an American-born Korean meant that there was no impossible dream—as long as one was willing to work for it.

Now, some 50 years after winning the second gold in platform diving, my bride of 52 years and I finally became grandparents four years, three years, and seven months ago; and I get to relive the golden moment every time I hug and kiss them.

—SAMMY LEE, M.D.
Olympic 2X Gold
Medalist, diving

Every day I try to make a masterpiece.

—PAT McCORMICK
Olympic 7X Gold
Medalist, Diving

I've had to ponder for awhile to select my best day as I have various chapters in m life and have been blessed with many great days.

As an athlete I must say my best day was the day I won the 1984 Olympic Sprint Kayak Trials. I changed on this day; no more doubts, only confidence, poise and maturity to challenge the world in three Olympic games.

I've coached volleyball, canoeing and kayaking. Every time an athlete comes to me and says I have had a positive influence on their life is a best day. I'm overwhelmed with pride and happiness for the individual.

I'm a new mommy. After years of infertility work the day my son was born is my best day and every day thereafter. I feel sooo lucky!

—SHEILA CONOVER DOYLE
3X Olympian, flat water kayaking

As promised, the following is a capsule of my best days - one in tennis and one in life: December 25, 1972 (in tennis): This was the day I won the Indian National Championship for the first time and became the best player in Asia, which I was for the next 15 years. It was also the day that my older brother, Anand, and I won the men's doubles and my younger brother, Ashk, won the junior singles. My parents were there and we came home with four titles on Christmas Day. We became the first family of tennis in my country. It was a magnificent day that I will never forget.

October 2, 1983 and November 3, 1987 (in life): These are the dates of my sons' births. Prakash was born on October 2 and Vikram on November 3. The first, I was away playing the Davis Cup for India in Tokyo and Prakash came two-weeks early. My wife was amazing to have her first child without me there. When I arrived at L.A. Airport and went straight to the hospital the feeling was one of amazement.

With my second son, I made sure I didn't do anything three-weeks before and after—making sure I was in town. They were wonderful days; and today my first son is 18 and my second son is 14. They are the best things that have ever happened to me.

—VIJAY AMRITRAJ
Professional Tennis Player

I always felt team competition was more reward-
ing than personal triumphs, so my best day came
in the Davis Cup competition. Representing Australia versus the United States in the Challenge
Round, 1964 in Cleveland. We were down 2-1,
losing the doubles to McKinely-Ralston. It was a
tough match; however, I felt I had let Roy Emerson
and Australia down. The next day I played Dennis
Ralston; led two sets to one; Dennis got back to
two sets all. He went up a break point in the fifth
set. The great Don Budge, a spectator, jumped up
yelling and screaming for Ralston. Captain Harry Hopman calmed me down and I came back to
win 6-4 in the fifth set. The next day Roy Emerson
beat Chuck McKinley and we took the Davis Cup
back to Australia—certainly a best day.

—**FRED STOLLE**
Professional Tennis Player

145

I have been blessed with so many I must give more than one.

Spiritually: When my friend Allan opened my eyes to the truths in the Bible.

Family-wise: That first night when I met my future wife, Cosette, and later when we had Josef, Erik and Matthew.

Athletically: When we won the bronze medal against a Cuban team, which we hadn't beaten for three years after watching our dreams of a second gold slip away the night before to Brazil.

And I could go on and on...

—ROBERT CTVRTLIK
Olympic 2X Gold Medalist,
Volleyball Player and member
of the International Olympic
Committee

My best day is every day—when I consider where I live, my loving family and great friendships and the fact that I wake up every morning to my beautiful wife Evelyn and daughter Kerstyn.

—BILL YARDLEY
USC volleyball player,
All-American

Ever the optimist, I would like to think that today is going to be my best day.

With regards to my storied baseball career, if you are a baseball fan my best day is obvious. It would be that October day in 1977, when I hit three home runs on three successive pitches in the World Series, taking the New York Yankees to the Championship and winning the Most Valuable Player Award.

One last thought: "unless you try to do something beyond what you have already mastered, you will never grow." I truly believe that my "best day" is yet to come and I hopes that you will strive to make everyday your best day.

—REGGIE JACKSON
Hall of Fame MLB Player;
New York Yankees, California
Angels, Oakland A's, 5X World
Series Champion, 2X WS MVP,
4X Home Run Leader

I guess I would have to say my best day would be when I proposed to my fiancée and she said, "of course." I have been lucky enough to have had many amazing days, but that one stands out.

—SHANE DORIAN
Professional Surfer

As any athlete who has ever competed can tell you, best days are in the eye of the beholder. Although as an oarsman I experienced many highs and lows, as a competitor (Collegiate, Nationally, Pan American Games and World Championships), the most singularly sublime athletic high I ever had was winning the Varsity Eights as the San Diego Crew Classic in April, 1982.

For the West Coast Rower this race meant 'the big time." Since it was my first significant victory and one achieved in record time over legendary crew powerhouses like Harvard, Yale and the University of Washington, just the thought of it to this day produces butterflies in my stomach.

I was at San Diego in later years as well as at other venues all over the world. However, if best day means the first time one is paid off for all of their hard work and dedication, than that sunny day at San Diego's Mission bay will forever be etched in my mind as first among great moments in my athletic career.

—CHRIS CLARK
Varsity Rowing Coach, University of Wisconsin

It is difficult to single out any one day as the best day in my life. I have been blessed to have a wonderful life filled with so many positive experiences. What I have tried to practice is a quotation from Will Rogers which states, "Make each day your masterpiece." This has worked well for me and helps me look at the bright side each day and see the good in almost all situations.

—GARY CUNNINGHAM

*Athletic Director, University of
California, Santa Barbara*

I will have to say that my best day came when we were trailing UCLA in the final two minutes of the game, 12-7. With both teams in 1969 being undefeated in the final game of the season, the winner would be going to the Rose Bowl. There was 1:32 left in the game, I caught a 32 yard touchdown pass to put us up 14-12. We went on to beat Michigan 10-3 in the 1970 Rose Bowl.

—SAM DICKERSON

USC Trojan Wide Receiver 1969

The day I got hired at Newport Harbor High School

—BILL BARNETT

NHHS Head Water Polo Coach

Winning the Kentucky Derby in 2005 aboard Giacamo was a dream

come true. It was the most humbling experience that I have ever felt. I thank God every day for blessing me with that day, my best day ever!

—MIKE SMITH

Jockey, ESPY Top Jockey, 1993,
National Museum of Racing
Hall of Fame 2003

It is hard to pick a "best day" from a long life, but professionally, it would have to be the day that I first earned a starting spot in the field for the Indianapolis 500 in 1977. That was the era of A.J. Foyt, Mario Andretti, Johnny Rutherford, and huge entries—as many as 90 cars trying to make a 33-car field. It changed my life!

—JANET GUTHRIE
Professional Race Car Driver,
International Motorsports Hall
of Fame 2006

My best Day was the day when I found out I made the Olympic Team the 1st time.

—CATHY RIGBY
1972 Gymnastic Olympian,
Actress, Peter Pan

My Best day? That is easy. June 11, 2012 (Kings won the Stanley Cup)

—DEAN LOMBARDI
President & General Manager;
Los Angeles Kings

It was difficult to decide on any one best day. Anyway, my Best Day was running track while in the Navy. It was great comradery with my mates and I always enjoyed the hurdles.

—GEORGIE KERR

I've had lots of good fortune in my lifetime, so there have been quite a few "best days" to consider, both on and off the golf course. Pressed to choose one, I guess it would be the day that I won the United States Amateur Championship That was Saturday, August 28, 1954, the date of the final round of our country's most prestigious amateur tournament at the Country Club of Detroit.

I was just short of 25 yreas old at the time, working as a paint salesman in Cleveland with the welcome opportunity to play a lot of golf as part of the job. I had enjoyed a fairly-successful career in my teen years and as a member of the Wake Forest College golf team. Then I spent three years in the Coast Guard, much of the time in Cleveland, where I was working when I qualified for the 1954 Amateur.

But, why was that August 28 my best day?

One obvious reason was the victory itself, but more importantly it convinced me that I had a future in professional golf, that my game was strong enough to compete successfully against the best pros in the word. A few months later, I turned pro and launched my career at the start of the 1955 season.

My first win on the PGA Tour came that year in the Canadian Open and I guess my decision was verified in subsequent seasons when I won 91 more tournaments, among them seven major championships. The Amateur victory truly was the turning point of my career and life.

—ARNOLD PALMER
All-time leader, PGA wins with 62, 4-time Masters Winner, 2-Time Open Winner, World Golf Hall of Fame 1974

It has always been a goal of mine to approach every day with the mindset that it was going to be my "best day". Utilizing this positive philosophy has directly made the frequency of so-called "bad days" occur few and far to none. Although I can fortunately think of many great days throughout my experiences, there is one day that stands out in my mind as holding memorable above all. This memorable day was experienced on the day of my younger sisters high school graduation. For so many, high school graduation is a special day that marks the end of an important chapter and the beginning of endless opportunities. For the reasons above, this day could be regarded as a "best day" for so many young individuals, and for some just an ordinary day that grants the freedom to move forward in their lives. My sister's high school graduation day was a day I will never forget, as it was a day that many people thoughts were uncertain would come, and uncertain if even a possibility. At six months of age, my sister had experienced a bad reaction to a vaccination, which caused her to have a major stroke and experience compulsive seizures. The result of the experience left my sister with major brain damage in the right side of her brain and severely handicapped. Consequently, my sister was going to need assistance with most of her daily operations for the rest of her life. Regardless of the restrictions my sister faces on a daily basis, she is the most loving, courageous, and happiest person I know. Watching my sister overcome multiple odds, walk without her wheelchair (with the assistance of her aide) down the graduation aisle, and sit alongside her classmates throughout her high school graduation ceremony, was an absolutely unforgettable and inspiration moment in my life. I anticipate endless best days in my future; however, this day will always reign above all in my book. My sister has taught me intangible lessons in life and has given me gifts that no other could provide, and it is not too often that she gets "her" moment in life to stand out and bask in her greatness. This special day has "her" day, and it was her moment to shine in her success alongside her peers. At this moment she knew she was the star, and the beaming smile on her face while walking down the graduation aisle is a heartfelt image I could never forget. I have absolutely no doubt that this "best day" in my life will continue to be my daily inspiration.

—**KRISTEN CASE**
*Men's and Women's Head
Tennis Coach, Newport Harbor
High School*

My best day has to be the first college volleyball match I ever started in. It wasn't until my senior year and I knew the 3 years prior, working my tail off as a walk on, was worth. I didn't have the best coach to player relationship with my volleyball coach freshman through junior year, but when my coach got hired for the off season of junior year to my senior season, I was ecstatic because I finally learned again what it felt like to be appreciated by my coach. After working my butt off all summer to prove to my new coach that I could start as a senior, I was 20 lbs lighter, much better at defense, and had an attitude that was so positive she gladly started me. My UCI women's volleyball team traveled to Reno to play in a tournament. Our very first match of our pre season was against Cal Berkeley, the 6th placed ranked team in the nation., Needless to say, as an unranked underdog team, we went into the match with a "nothing to lose, everything to gain" attitude. We warmed up 45 minutes before game time and when coach announced the starting lineup and I heard number 5, my number, get called into the starting lineup, I almost fainted. I never showed her how nervous I was but as much as she knew, she still had faith in me. I was confident enough to go out there and stare these Cal Bears in the face. From the first point to the very end, I was in a zone. No mistake was too big and no good play was good enough. We kept our heads and kept working and working. Cal took the first game and we took the 2nd and 3rd game, they came back to win a close 4th game and all we had left to decide the match was the 5th game to 15. I have never been part of such fun game; we won the 5th game and beat up the Bears. We took a 13-9 lead and I had one of my favorite saves in this match. We closed out the 5th and celebrated like we had just won a National Championship. Even though the rest of the season never measured up to that game, I will never forget that my first match I ever started in for Division 1 volleyball in college would be my last year of eligibility against a top 10 nationally ranked team. I still have the DVD and watch it every now and then when I get reminiscent of volleyball. I loved that match, I loved our team, and I love looking back on it still. This just shows that through all the stormy struggles, there is going to be sunlight one day and everything else that once was the "worst" thing to experience, doesn't matter. I also forget to mention that when I was working in the off season of my junior year, I wanted to quit because I couldn't finish sprints in conditioning. My new head coach Paula watched as I struggled, nearly quit, and somehow dug deep to finish 3rd in the last set of sprints we did and from then on, she never let me give up on myself. I would have never known what it was like to overcome adversity, and I will never forget that.

—LAUREN SOTO
UCI Volleyball

My Best Day has not come yet!

—PETER UEBERROTH
*Commissioner of Baseball,
1984 Los Angeles Summer
Olympics Organizer*

Every day for 50 plus years that I put on a Professional Baseball uniform.

—TONY LA RUSSA
*MLB Player, Kansas City
Athletics, Chicago Cubs, MLB
Manager, Oakland Athletics, St
Louis Cardinals Member, Base-
ball Hall of Fame 2014*

Sandy Cameron, my father and former 1939 UCLA teammate of Jackie Robinson, took my brother and me to a 1963 UCLA basketball game. It must have been the old Men's Gym or maybe the L.A. Sports Arena, given Pauley Pavilion had yet to be built. I was 9 years old. After the Bruin win we were invited to the locker room and my father had brought along a new "leather" basketball. Coach Wooden, Gail, Walt, Keith, Jack, Kenny, Fred and all of the boys put their names to that ball. For me, it was the beginning of a lifelong love affair with the game of basketball.

The next day, with my Dad at work and I on the asphalt drive way, that ball began its long, up and down journey. The ball, of course, began to scuff and the names began to fade. Who would have thought that the undefeated '63-64 UCLA Bruin would be the first of a string of Coach Wooden championship teams? When my dad came home, he kind of winced but said, "keep playing". And I did. And later in life a became a teacher and coach. That ball, is a way, became my life. It no longer exists except as a priceless memory of my best day.

—SCOTT CAMERON
Ensign Intermediate School/
Teacher and Coach

Gene has Alzheimer's so he is unable to contribute. Of course, his "best day" in his career was winning the Championship 1-2-1957. In his life there were many. He is doing very well at this time.

—GENE FULLMER,
(AS TOLD BY HIS FAMILY)
Professional Boxer,
Middleweight

Surfing every day in Kauai

—ALANA BLANCHARD
Professional Surfer

In High School, in those days they didn't draft you. They approached you, if the team liked you. The problem with that in the old days was that if you signed over 4K you went straight to the major leagues with no experience. Only about 5 or 6 guys would do that. Killebrew, Koufax, Al Kaline, etc. did that. I was signing out of high school and I wanted experience. I was approached by the New York Yankees, Dodgers, and Cincinnati & Philly-no draft. I worked out with them-and the Yankees said I could workout with them during home stands. I got to hit with the big guys, Yogi Berra, Mickey Mantle, Bobby Richardson, Elson Howard, Moose Gower, Whitey Ford-and I worked out. Malcom Patterson from the Dodgers came by too. Malcom found out I was going to sign with the Yankees on a Tuesday night, he had Jackie Robinson call me the Sunday night before the Yankees wanted me to sign Tuesday night. I signed Tuesday afternoon with the Dodgers!

— TOMMY DAVIS
MLB Player, L.A. Dodgers, Houston Astros, Baltimore Orioles, 3-Time All Star, 2-Time NL Batting Champion

Other than each of the days when my sons were born, I'd have to say my best day was when I won the Indianapolis 500 in 1963 which would then obviously be "my best sports day."

—PARNELLI JONES
Professional Race Car Driver, International Motorsports Hall of Fame 1990. 1961 Indianapolis co-Rookie of the Year

Whenever I had a serious injury or set back, I use the Lord to find his strength and encouragement to get through it.

My best day was seeing our children being born! Winning the Stanley Cup and being with my family was also a highlight. Those are cherished memories you can never get back...

—GLEN WESLEY
Professional Hockey Player,
Boston Bruins, Toronto
Maple Leafs

I am pleased to let you know that my best day was September 21, 1990 the day that my son, Ross Tyler Summit, was born. All the months of anticipation culminated in the most wonderful day of my life. His birth has changed and fulfilled my life in so many ways--ways that only a mother can describe. I thank God for him each and every day, and I count him as my greatest achievement in life.

—PAT SUMMITT
Head Basketball Coach, 8X
NCAA Division I Champions
University of Tennessee

My best day so far is April 2ns, 2014—the day that I became the head coach at Louisiana Tech. That day showed me that God truly had a plan and a purpose for me to be a head coach and glorify Him through coaching. It was an honor to take over a such a prestigious program and to work for Athletics Director Tommy McClelland and Dr. Guice, our President.

My wife, AnDe, was with me the entire day. She sacrificed many things in her life to make it possible for me to become a head coach. It was a joy having her with me as we started a new chapter of our lives. We were able to discuss buying our first home and moving from Wisconsin to Louisiana-a scary yet exciting time for a young couple in their early 20's.

MY parents were able to come to my press conference on April 2nd. It was meaningful to have them there on such a special day because they always supported me as I pursued my goals.

I was able to announce Mickie DeMoss as our associate head coach. Mickie was in the hospital room when I was born and has been a family to me ever since. I was so grateful that she chose to move to Ruston and help me. Mickie and I also began discussing our staff at LA Tech—a staff that I now, over a year later, consider my family.

I believe that life is about relationship-both with God and the people around us. April 2nd, 2014 was a day for me to celebrate the relationships I had established and also to start building new relationships that have become more fulfilling than I could imagine.

—TYLER SUMMITT
LA Tech Womens's
Basketball Coach

I have been coaching youth volleyball now in the Orange County, CA area for over 14 years. I have coached at 5 different high schools, boys & girls club and have been a volunteer assistant at the University of California, Irvine. There have been some amazing matches I have been involved with, both on the good side and bad side of the outcome. The relationships I have built with my players over the years is what I cherish most about coaching these young adults. However, through all my coach experiences my best day came on July 2nd, 2009/

The process started back in the fall of 2008. I was coaching and still am at OCVBC, running the 14 and under group of about 50 girls. We practice starting in December, and after 4 months, my 14 Blue team was established. We practice 3-4 days a week, and have tournaments about every 4 weeks. Everything was building up to the largest annual youth sporting event in the world, the Volleyball Festival in Phoenix, AZ. This is where 8,000 girls from 12-18 years old would participate in a week long tournament that would finish in the US Airways Center where the NBA Basketball team the Phoenix Suns and the WNBA Mercury play.

The OCVBC 14 Blue team played well all week, winning all of their matches and losing only one game in the tournament. After beating the reigning champs,

Puerto Rico in the round before the quarter finals, our starting opposite right side player tore some ligaments in her ankle in a freak accident celebrating with her teammates. Although we were playing well, our chances to reach our goal looked a little dim. The other ten girls really stepped up and played with a lot of heart to beat two very good teams to reach the Finals. Out of 103 teams, only one more stood in our way to the title.

I remember the day like it was yesterday. What we had for breakfast, walking into the arena for the first time, and seeing the expressions on the girls faces when I took them on the floor where we would play before we went to the locker room for our pre-game talk. When we walked into the locker room, they had their names on place cards over each locker. It was pretty exciting for 13 & 14 year old girls. heck, it was pretty exciting for a 39 year old coach. One Thirty had come and it was time to head out to the court to warm up.

As we were warming up, I remember how nervous I was. I thought to myself if I was this nervous, how were the girls feeling? The format was 2 out of 3. The first two games were played to 25 and the third, if necessary, was played to 15. The first game was a blur. The girls were scared, nervous, and were like deer in head lights. I tried everything, but it didn't matter. We ended up losing that first game pretty bad. The second game was different. As I was turning in my lineup, I looked over and saw one of my Captains getting in the faces of the other girls. She was fired up and wanted to light a fire under the girls she had battled with all year long. She rallied them to a dominating win in game two. It came down to the third and final game. It went back and forth. I remember the crowd starting to get louder and louder. It seemed everyone was standing from about 12-12 on. Past 15 we went. We had match point, then they had it. Momentum kept switching sides. Then, finally at 21-20 we dug a driven ball perfectly to the setter where she set our middle blocker and she put the ball away. As the girls dog piled in the center court, I stood there with my assistant coach just watching the joy and excitement that these girls have worked so hard for the last ten months. I was so proud of these girls. As I hugged the girls, parents and other coaches from our club, I remember tears running down my face. During my coaching career, this was by far my best day.

—SCOTT BRUCE
OCVBC Volleyball Coach

My best day was March 27, 2015. This is the date I, my staff, and my Division II college women's basketball team won the NCAA National Championship in Sioux Falls, South Dakota. I would assume this would be the most obvious best day for a great deal of coaches who were in their fourth year as head coach. Of for someone who is only 31 years old. It seems to be the pinnacle of any coaches career and a very difficult and sometimes seemingly unattainable feat.

For me, this day represented something much bigger though. My team had been through the most devastating loss of their lives on January 18th the same year. One of our own, a senior on our team, passed away suddenly and unexpectedly. The emotional rollercoaster these young women were on for the rest of the season is unexplainable. There were moments of complete sadness to times of extreme anger. There was a lack of focus coupled with an intensity to finish the season for our Shanice. The determination and strength these young people showed and the perseverance they displayed to not only finish the season, but to emerge as champions was unheard of. They are holding that trophy, "we are the Champions" plays in the background, and tears of joy streams from their eyes, they chant Shanice's name at center court and hold up the #44 with both hands. This is MY best day because it was THEIR best day and certainly one day I will never forget.

— JESSICA STORM
*Head Women's Basketball
Coach, California University
of Pennsylvania*

Today is my best day. It is not just an issue of yesterday being past and tomorrow being guaranteed. It is, rather that today is the day that I have to improve upon both that which I did well and that which I did poorly. My 65 years have brought with them the wisdom that while the past (and its memories, experiences, and it achievements) has its priority and the future has its hopes and promises, life exists in the moment. Life is far too precious a gift for us to simply allow it to be something that's happening to us while we're doing something else—even if that "something else" is reliving past great experiences and achievements.

—HARRY EDWARDS

University of California, Berkley
Sociologist; "The Revolt of the
Black Athlete"; Staff Consultant
SF 49ers, Golden State Warriors

My Best Day? Actually Days- the two days my children were born!

Watching my daughters Carolyn and Finley come into the world- what could be better than that?

My best career day would be one that reoccurs every year.

The 24 hours stretch of calling the NCAA National Championship Game and then hours later arriving at Augusta National to begin preparation for the Masters.

—JIM NANTZ
CBS Sporstscaster; NFL, College Basketball, PGA Tour

I believe everyday is our best day, and if we wake up in the morning God has given us a chance to make it our best day. Make every day count.

My "best day" begins with the privilege of coaching the Freshman Basketball team at Newport Harbor High School, in Newport Beach, CA. My first year coaching High School basketball was the Freshman basketball season of 2006. Before the league season began that year we were scheduled to play some non-league games and two tournaments. The first tournament we played we won our first two games. I thought to myself, what a great start, I think we have a pretty good team. And we did. Our third game we went up against a very strong team from Santa Margarita Catholic High School, a private school that has a very strong tradition in basketball in S CA. Not knowing much about this team and being a new high school coach, I thought "how good can they be?" they are just freshmen like my team. Well, how wrong I was. The game was a clinic, that is for us watching it. They went around us, over us, through us and into us. They went by us for lay-ups, jump shots, three point shots and even a freshman dunked on us. We lost by over thirty points and were never in it. OK, now my "best day" begins.

Fast forward a couple of weeks and our head coach tells me we have a non-league game vs Mira Costa at home. No problem, He continues to say he made a mistake on the schedule and this game was the same day as the semi-finals of a tournament we are playing in. Two games in one day! Yikes! One game at home at 3:00 pm and one game one hour away by car at 6:00pm. We had won our first three games of the tournament to make it into the semi-finals and this is why we had a conflict. We decided to play both games with this plan in mind: The first game at 3:00pm at home we would play the first team (seven players) for the first half and play the second half with the second team (eight players). The second team players would stay and finished the game. With a one point lead at half-time we jumped into the bus with seven players and headed to the tournament game at 6pm. You can guess by now who we are playing in the second game, yes, that same "pro team" Santa Margarita that hammered us a couple of weeks before. This time we would be ready and warmed up (from the first half game) to play at a completely different level. This was "my best day" because I watched a group of kids that believed they could rise to the challenge to compete with a team that was bigger, better, faster and stronger. The difference was clear from the opening tip, these seven kids came to play their hearts out and it showed. With a very focused attach, they went up against this team and out rebounded them, out hustled them and executed to perfection on offenses to win the game by over thirty points. It was my "best day" watching these seven kids play to their highest potential. And yes. they did go on to win the Championship the next evening. This is the best day you could ever have as a coach.

—GREG D BROWN
NHHS Basketball Coach

I think when you as about my best day, it certainly wasn't on the football field. I played football for 12 years, and I had broken my Achilles tendon and I was basically lost. I was divorced and I was going out on a trip when an airline stewardess told me about a man who taught the bible on TV, his name was Apostle Fred Price. I walked away from her, but she came back and asked me for my phone number, so I gave it to her.

Sunday morning, my phone rang, and a man named Ken Ludwig called saying, "my wife told me to call you to watch the man on TV who teaches the bible, Fred Price". I said, "I don't know a Ken Ludwig," but he told me that his wife told him to call me. Ken Ludwig told me to turn on channel 11 at 8:30 to listen to the man speak on the bible. It was an almighty great day for me, because I called my son and we both listened.

One Saturday night, soon after, my son asked me to take him to church, and I told him that I didn't want to go to church. My son said, "But dad, I have never been to Church." Of course that put a pain in my heart, so I said we will go one day, and so we went. We heard the gospel of Jesus Christ, how he died on a cross to forgive us for our sins and gave us our right to become a member of the family of God by asking him into our hearts. It changed my life, and it's never been the same. It helps me to become a better person every day because he said, "He'll never leave us nor forsake us (John 3:16)

—ROOSEVELT "Rosey" GRIER

Defensive Tackle, NY Giants, LA Rams 2X Pro Bowler, 3X All-Pro Team

I have been so fortunate to get to do what I love for my entire life. As a dad, my "best day" was any day I was able to watch our 3 kids play sports and see them have fun while competing. Nothing better than that.

As a coach, my best day was when our teams had that "AHA" moment and came together to achieve our main goal. The main goal is to always reach our full potential. Yes, it was nice to win titles but that was not always "my best day"; the interaction with the kids and seeing them grow as people and players are what make my "best day."

—TOM PESTOLESI
Irvine Valley College
Volleyball Coach

My Best Day:

1) Super Bowl XVI

2) Stanford 33- Notre Dame 16

—BILL WALSH
Hall of Fame NFL Coach, LA Raiders, San Diego Chargers, SF 49ers; 3X Super Bowl Championship; College Head Coach, Stanford University, 1977 Pac 8 Coach of the Year

My amateur career was very limited-no high school golf team existed in the 1940's.

however, after transferring from two years at U.C. Santa Barbara to Cal Berkeley, and losing one year by rules I played on enjoyable year at Cal. My highlight is our 18 hole matches was defeating Ken Venturi of San Jose State. As a pro I did finish 2nd to Bud Holscher in the 1960 State Open.

From a coaching career with my son, Sammy, there were many highlights-from winning the Junior World, making the cut in the L.A. Open at age 17, to being runner-up in the U.S. Amateur in 1984 and then winning in 1985. However, the most memorable one moment was during the 1985 Masters playing with Jack Nicklaus in the 3rd round on #15. Sammy followed Jack's short chip for an eagle with his 10 foot eagle putt following an excellent 7 iron 2nd shot. I'll never forget Jacks thumbs up & wink he gave Sammy. This helped him win the first of his 2 low amateur awards.

All this and his excellent U.S.C. career (13 wins) resulted in his induction into the USC Hall of Fame.

—SAM RANDOLPH, SR
Golfer & Head Pro at La Cumbe
Country Club, University of
California at Berkeley

My best day at USC was in the spring of 1985 at the Fresno State Classic. I played the best tournament of my Trojan career; shooting 16 under par and winning the individual title by 10 shots! When I got to the 18th green in the last group I found out we were 1 shot behind UCLA and Fresno State for the team title. I had a 50 foot putt with 10 feet of break and somehow made it to tie the Bruins & Bulldogs.

Two weeks later I had the privilege to play in my first Masters Tournament. I made the cut playing with Tom Watson on Friday. Then I got paired with Jack Nicklaus on Saturday. We both shot 72 and I got paired with him again on Sunday. I finished 18th and won the low amateur award. It doesn't get much better that that for a twenty year old. I finished the season winning the Fred Haskins award for best college player and went on to win the U.S. Amateur later that summer. What great memories! I'm proud to be a Trojan then and forever!

—SAM RANDOLPH JR

University of Southern California, Golfer, 13 college victories and USC Hall of Fame 2005; U.S. Amateur Champion 1985, PGA Tour Winner 1987,

About the Author:

Mark Keys is a Southern California native, residing in Costa Mesa with his wife Laurie, daughters, Page and Megan, their dog, Fumble, and two cats, Lucy and Ethel. Mark loves that his mom still lives at the beach in Newport in the house he grew up in, and he spends a lot of time there with her & the girls and walking the beach. He played basketball growing up, in High School, and beyond as well as body surfed until he injured his back. Mark is an avid reader, enjoys watching classic movies & westerns, collecting film and sports memorabilia, walking and listening to Jazz, Motown & Rat Pack music, and hanging out with friends. He also loves to travel and going to sporting events & college practices, when health permits. In spite of thousands of hours of physical therapy and his numerous surgeries, including 6 back, 9 ankle, 9 knee, and 2 shoulder surgeries, he also experienced shingles, pneumonia, MRSA Staph infection, prostate infection, concussions, he has no immune system and fights continuous headaches and other health issues every day. But, through all of this, he keeps a positive attitude and outlook to make each day, his best day.

28926670R00109

Made in the USA
San Bernardino, CA
11 January 2016